CW00696017

From

_____

Date

_____

Message

_____

_____

_____

_____

Y SECONDS WITH GOD by Ron Hembree

© 1999 Christian Art Gifts, RSA

Copyright © 1975 by Ron Hembree. Originally published under
the title *Sixty Seconds with God* by Baker Books, a division of
Baker Book House Company, Grand Rapids, Michigan, 49516,
USA. All rights reserved.

First edition 1999
Second edition 2006

Designed by Christian Art Gifts

Scripture taken from the *Holy Bible*, King James Version.
Copyright © 1962 by The Zondervan Corporation. Used by
permission.

Printed in China

ISBN 978-1-86920-594-2

© All rights reserved. No part of this book may be reproduced
in any form without permission in writing from the publisher,
except in the case of brief quotations embodied in critical ar-
ticles or reviews.

07 08 09 10 11 12 13 14 15 16 - 14 13 12 11 10 09 08 07 06 05

SIXTY SECONDS
with GOD

RON HEMBREE

christian
art gifts.

Preface

It is not uncommon for corporations to pay $80 000 to air a one-minute advertisement on television. Even in a society known for its inflation this is a lot of money for just sixty seconds. Executives know, however, just what one minute of communication can do to sell their products. They consider such expenditures reasonable if not inexpensive.

In religious circles we have always placed greater value on the quantity of time spent praying than on the quality. But Jesus said, "when ye pray, use not vain repetitions, as the heathen do: for they think that they shall be heard for their much speaking" (Matt. 6:7). This does not make it any less necessary to get alone with God for long stretches of time, but neither should we ever forget the value of our minutes with God. This book was written to make each minute with God count. Each devotion can be read in sixty seconds, and this should be helpful to busy people. I pray that this book will bless you and that all of us will increase our appreciation of every moment we spend communing with and meditating on our Lord.

Bucket of water

"Ask, and it shall be given you;
seek and ye shall find; knock,
and it shall be opened unto you."
MATTHEW 7:7

In the middle of a lake near Akron, Ohio, is
an island that was once the site of a famous
amusement park. Shortly after the park lodge
was first constructed one hundred years ago,
it caught fire. Fire fighters rowed to the island
to fight the blaze. A candy vendor working
on shore wanted to do his part, so he filled a
bucket with water, rowed to the island, tossed
it on the burning structure, and rowed back
to shore for more water. It never occurred to
him to use the lake water.

While we laugh at the candy vendor, many
men try to solve their problems in much the

same way. Divine help is available, but they ignore it and struggle to solve the human dilemma with human wisdom. After all their exhausting efforts the fire still burns and little is accomplished.

If we question this premise, we need only look at the recidivism rates in our prison system. Sixty to ninety percent of those coming out will return within five years. Yet we still try to rehabilitate without a spiritual perspective. How much wiser we would be to dip deeply into the resources Christ offers to change men. This is true not only with the problems of our society, but also with our personal needs.

Show the way

Then the devil leaveth him, and, behold, angels came and ministered unto him.
MATTHEW 4:11

Appalled by the rising illiteracy rate in the United States, the government decided to launch a campaign to get people to read. One of the brainstorms of the official campaign was to place a sign in all the buses of San Francisco: "Illiterate? Write today for free help." Needless to say, the campaign did not improve matters much, because those who needed to read the sign could not.

God understood from the beginning that posting signs for spiritually illiterate people will not suffice. Therefore, He planned to send His own Son into the world to show men how to live. Christ then died and rose again so men could be free from the power of sin and death. No other way would work. Earthlings simply could not read and understand the signs of the Law or the Prophets. They had to be shown. So Christ came.

Looking at the earthly life of our Lord, we learn so much about how to live. We can learn one of the most powerful lessons from the way in which He handled temptation. Satan attacked Him when He was weak and hungry. Yet Christ rebuffed the attacks of Satan by skillful use of God's eternal Word. Against such testimony Satan does not have a chance. Let us today look closely at every situation in the life of our Lord and learn how we too are to act and react.

Heart to heart

Now the end of the commandment is charity out of a pure heart, and of a good conscience, and of faith unfeigned.
1 TIMOTHY 1:5

Ralph Waldo Emerson lovingly visited the grave of his young wife every day for two years after her death. And though he was one of the greatest intellects of the day, ordinary people learned to love him for his sentiment and honesty. One New Englander said, "We are a simple folk here, but we understand Mr. Emerson because he speaks our language." And he did speak their language. His lofty ideas and deep intellect never were wasted in arrogance or conceit.

In his letter to young Timothy, Paul insisted that Timothy always speak to the hearts of the people. He said some false teachers who had come into the church delighted in using high-sounding words and impressing everyone with their knowledge. Timothy was never to do this. Rather his life and lips must overflow with love, a good conscience, and a genuine faith.

Each of us has a specific work to do for our Lord. Perhaps yours is to teach or occasionally preach. Most likely it is just to share Christ with friends one-on-one. It is vital that we remember Paul's exhortation to speak to people's hearts. We need not impress them with our great knowledge; we need only touch them with our love.

Improving the preacher

*I exhort therefore, that, first of all,
supplications, prayers, intercessions,
and giving of thanks, be made for all men.*
1 TIMOTHY 2:1

The Scottish pastor John Carmichael, serving his first church, was young and very frightened. He felt that he was doing badly and that his people were looking at him with pity and contempt. One day, to his terror, the stern elders of the flock filed into his vestry. "Next Sabbath," they told him, "before you begin to speak, we ask you to say to yourself, 'They're all loving me.' And it's true, we will all be loving you very much." That meeting changed the young preacher's life, and today he is recognized as one of the finest preachers Scotland ever produced.

Paul understood the pressures of the pastorate. He also understood that people could be a tremendous blessing to young Timothy as he tried to lead the church at Ephesus. Therefore, Paul told Timothy to admonish the people first of all to pray for their leaders. Praying people produce good pastors.

This advice is still good. And it goes for all men in positions of leadership. Before we criticize them, judge their actions, or disagree with their decisions, we are first to pray for them, intercede on their behalf, and thank God for them. We must always temper our complaints with prayers. May we pledge today to pray, as God's Word demands, for all those in authority.

Hope

*According to his abundant mercy God
hath begotten us again unto a lively hope.*
1 PETER 1:3

Several years ago serious lung cancer threatened the life of entertainer Arthur Godfrey. Godfrey says, "Over the years I've developed a pretty good sense of optimism – even about the weather. 'What a lousy day,' people sometimes gripe. Not me. When you've lived as long as I have, and survived as much, every day you draw breath is borrowed time and, therefore, a great day." Godfrey's attitude is a healthy one because, as writer John Buchanan says, "Without optimism there can be no vitality."

Earthly optimism may relieve some tensions. There comes a time, however, when even this cannot carry man beyond the barrier he faces. This is where spiritual optimism comes in. The Bible calls it hope. Hope is one of the three graces of the Holy Spirit: "And now abideth faith, hope, charity, these three … " (1 Cor. 13:13).

While the greatest of the graces is love, hope still has a vital role in the life of the believer. And God's Word tells us to hope for three things: God's calling (Eph. 1:18), eternal life (Col. 1:5), and the resurrection (Acts 23:6). Believers are to be optimistic. Our lives do not end at the grave. And we are assured that "all things work together for good to them that love God, to them who are the called according to His purpose" (Rom. 8:28).

Invisible cages

———— ·⟳· ————

For he shall have judgment without mercy,
that hath shewed no mercy; and mercy
rejoiceth against judgment.
JAMES 2:13

Birds live in invisible cages. While we often say someone is "free as a bird," all birdwatchers know that the conduct of birds is rigidly fixed. They are prisoners of the land they fly over and slaves to the air they fly through.

John and Jean George told of a wild cardinal they saw die because he could not break through this invisible barrier. He was strangled on a piece of property that was cleared of trees and plowed under. They said, "Almost all birds live and love and die behind bars of nature's compulsions. They are captives in cages of their own instincts, from which, with rare exceptions, they cannot escape."

Birds are not the only creatures locked behind invisible prison bars. James tells us that some people are lost through bitterness. He plainly says we can obtain mercy from God only as we are merciful: "For He shall have judgment without mercy, that hath shewed no mercy ... " On the other hand those who have learned to forgive are free because "mercy rejoiceth against judgment."

Those locked in the invisible prison of an unforgiving spirit will never be free. Those who have sought forgiveness from Christ, however, have found they first must forgive. In letting go of their anger they find real freedom. Forgive someone today.

Liberated

---

*Being confident of this very thing, that he
which hath begun a good work in you will
perform it until the day of Jesus Christ.*

PHILIPPIANS 1:6

Michelangelo saw the task of the sculptor
as that of freeing figures from their marble
prisons. In each block of stone he saw some
"person", and he chipped away until that form
emerged. Sometimes he failed, as with St. Matthew. This famous statue is only half finished
because Michelangelo could not get the stone
to release the figure of the brilliant apostle.

Paul saw God as the Sculptor who is freeing men from the prisons of their carnal natures. He wrote to the Philippians that God
was doing a great work in and on their lives
and encouraged them to have confidence in

18

His work. He assured the new believers that God is perfectly capable of "finishing" us as He desires for His and our greatest good. This master Sculptor never gives up, and no prison is too strong for His skilled eye and learned hand.

In yielding ourselves to the direction of the Master, we are "being filled with the fruits of righteousness, which are by Jesus Christ, unto the glory and praise of God" (Phil. 1:11). All believers should remember that today's bumps and bruises may merely be the Master chiseling, working away at our lives until we are conformed to the image of His Son. Thus we relax even though the chisel may bite, for we know His work is sure and the result to be well worth the moment's inconvenience.

London on fire

For I know that this shall turn to my
salvation through your prayer, and
the supply of the Spirit of Jesus Christ.
PHILIPPIANS 1:19

Fire raged for five days through the wooden structures of London, burning 13 000 buildings, including 89 churches, and doing thirty million dollars worth of damage. The death toll was staggering in that disaster about 315 years ago. Although the memory of London's holocaust has faded, it brought sweeping changes which still affect us today, changes like building codes, fire-insurance companies, and fire protection and prevention.

Pain most often brings change. Paul recognized this. In Philippians 1 he talked about people who were preaching with impure motives and bringing him personal pain. Yet he was confident that from this bad situation two things would occur: first, the name of Christ would be heard by many who had not heard it before; next, the Philippians would earnestly pray and that would bring many blessings to them, the church, and Paul.

Just as did the London fire, Paul's sufferings made people aware of the need for preventional protection; they were awakened to their tasks. On this day we would be wise to remember our priorities. Let us also pray that the gospel will be preached around the world.

Legend of fear

And in nothing be terrified by your adversaries.
PHILIPPIANS 1:28

An ancient legend of India tells of the "spirit of plague" passing an old man sitting under a tree. The man asked the spirit, "Where are you going?" The spirit answered, "To Benares to kill one hundred people." Later the man heard that ten thousand had died in that city. When the "spirit of plague" came back again, the man said to him, "You lied! You said you would only kill one hundred people." "I killed but one hundred," replied the spirit, "fear killed the rest."

Paul says much about fear. He told Timothy, "For God hath not given us the spirit of fear; but of power, and of love, and of a sound mind" (2 Tim. 1:7). And he reminded the

Philippians not to be terrified of their adversaries (1:28). Although the enemies of Christ might make believers uncomfortable physically, they cannot destroy the eternal soul. Believers need not panic in the face of pain or threat.

Ever practical, Paul specified things the Philippian believers were to do: first, their behavior was to be becoming to the gospel; then, they were to stand together in the faith as one body and to strive for the gospel. This is excellent advice for us in our strife-filled world. May we bring glory to the gospel, stand together in love, and constantly seek to be better Christians.

Death sentence

Look not every man on his own things,
but every man also on the things of others.
PHILIPPIANS 2:4

Loo Ching migrated to the United States from China several years ago, and soon after his arrival he violated a fundamental law of the Tong Soon. The council met and sentenced him to death, but American laws forbade the sentence to be carried out. So the leaders simply decreed Loo Ching a dead man.

From then on no one spoke to him. Shopkeepers would not sell him food. Children turned the other way when he came down the street. His room was rented to another and his belongings put in the alley. He could not speak English and knew nothing of American ways. Each day he grew thinner until one morning he was found dead in the snow outside a teashop.

People need people. In the tragic case of Loo Ching, his death sentence was effectively carried out when people withdrew their love. Paul says relationships are important. He encourages believers to consider others in everything they do. One can never withdraw his love from others and remain a believer.

"Am I my brother's keeper?" Paul tells us we are to be concerned for others. He also reminds us to hold others in higher esteem than we do ourselves. In other words, we are to invest our love and concern to those about us. We must remember that our Christian responsibility is both vertical and horizontal: to God and to others.

Forget the face

—— ✐ ——

Let this mind be in you, which
was also in Christ Jesus.
PHILIPPIANS 2:5

Charles William Eliot, one of the great presidents of Harvard University, was born with a serious facial disfigurement. Once he was old enough to be sensitive about it, his mother said, "My son, it is not possible for you to get rid of this handicap. We have consulted the best physicians and they can do nothing for you. But it is possible, with God's help, to grow a soul and mind so big that people will forget to look at your face." This was exactly what he did, and today he is recognized as one of the educators who shaped modern secondary education.

Paul talked about the only begotten Son

of God willfully coming to earth and humbling Himself to become a man. He further subjected Himself to the disfigurement of the cross. Yet Christ lived so purely and died so obediently that today we no longer remember the shame of the cross. Rather, His life, death, and resurrection force us to look beyond the ugliness to the glory of His salvation. One day every knee will bow before this Lord of lords.

Christ is our example of obedience. The challenge is clear. Our lives are to bring glory to His name. Paul said, "Let this mind be in you, which was also in Christ Jesus." We, like Eliot, can live lives so beautiful and meaningful that people will look beyond our human form to see the living Christ within us. May that be our prayer for this day.

Direct order

Do all things without
murmurings and disputings.
PHILIPPIANS 2:14

A cantankerous old lady came through surgery with flying colors. The surgeon sternly told her when she awoke, "In accordance with the rules of this hospital, you will have to walk ten minutes the very first day, and you will be out of here in a week since hospital beds are at a premium." On her first day the old woman took her steps as ordered and within a few days was walking all over the hospital. Later her family tried to pay the doctor a bonus for his work.

"Nonsense," he said. "It was just a routine operation."

"It's not the operation we're marveling

over," said the grandson. "It's her walking. She hasn't taken a step in sixty years!"

Some people apparently respond to direct and firm orders. In his Philippian letter Paul gave several direct orders to leave no room for argument. One of the sharpest was "Do all things without murmurings and disputings." This advice is not always easy to take, but it is Holy Scripture.

Paul said "all things." This means not only religious things, but even menial tasks of the day such as washing dishes, mowing the lawn, and carrying out the trash. Paul said we must obey this order so "that ye may be blameless and harmless, the sons of God, without rebuke, in the midst of a crooked and perverse nation, among whom ye shine as lights in the world" (Phil. 2:15).

Used and abused

For all seek their own, not the
things which are Jesus Christ's.
PHILIPPIANS 2:21

Cherub-faced Bobby Driscoll won the hearts
of Americans in the Walt Disney movie *Song
of the South*. His life ended in tragedy, however, when his body was found in March 30,
1968, in an abandoned tenement. Beside him
were empty beer bottles. He had died from
years of drug abuse. Shortly before his death at
age thirty-one, Bobby said, "I was carried on a
silver platter and then dumped into a garbage
can." He was bitter because those who liked
him as a child actor cared nothing for him
when he could no longer entertain them.

Too often men traffic in human flesh,
seeking what people have or are rather than

genuinely loving them. Paul noted that two men who traveled with him sincerely loved the people of Philippi. Of Timothy Paul said, "For I have no man likeminded, who will naturally care for your state." Of Epaphroditus Paul wrote, "For he longed after you all." These men really cared for people.

Most people in our world are reaching out for sincere friends. They need people who love them as they are rather than for what they have or for their prominent positions. Believers must see people as people, being neither awed nor appalled at their veneer. Today let us form lasting and loving friendships as did Timothy and Epaphroditus.

To make a mirror

—— ✎ ——

For we are the circumcision, which worship
God in the spirit, and rejoice in Christ Jesus,
and have no confidence in the flesh.
PHILIPPIANS 3:3

Madame Chaing Kai-shek tells of a young Buddhist monk two thousand years ago who looked pious, clasped his hands, and chanted "Amita Buddha" all day, believing he could thus acquire grace. One day the Father Prior of the temple sat beside him and began rubbing a piece of stone against a brick. This went on for several days until the young monk asked, "Father Prior, what are you doing?"

"I'm trying to make a mirror," he replied.

"But," protested the youth, "you cannot make a mirror of a brick."

"That is true," the old man replied, "and it

is just as impossible for you to attain grace by chanting all day."

This ancient Chinese story points to the truth that sinners cannot become saints unless their character changes. Paul understood this and frankly told the Philippians to have no confidence in the flesh, that is, not to consider themselves worthy of salvation because they had gone to the right schools, memorized the right things, and chanted the right prayers. Paul learned this from personal experience, because he had done all these things and they had not saved him.

Salvation is a divine interruption in man's heart. In Christ we are made new creatures and become totally dependent not on our own fleshy righteousness but on His grace. As the songwriter said, "Jesus paid it all, all to Him I owe."

Prophetic poem

*If by any means I might attain unto
the resurrection of the dead.*
PHILIPPIANS 3:11

After Dag Hammarskjöld's untimely death in an airplane crash, friends found a prophetic poem in his family Bible. Hammarskjöld had translated it when but a schoolboy. The poem simply said:

> The day you were born, everybody
> was happy – you cried alone.
> Make your life such, that in your
> last hour all others are weeping,
> And you are the only one
> without a tear to shed!
> Then you shall calmly face
> death, whenever it comes.

Hammarskjöld so lived, and the world wept at his passing.

Preoccupied with Christ's resurrection, Paul seemed to stretch so he might be worthy of the great price paid for his salvation. He admitted that he had not yet attained a state of perfection, but said he was seeking daily to be led by the Spirit and to grow in the Lord. He added that he forgot past mistakes and failures, and pressed on "toward the mark of the prize of the high calling of God in Christ Jesus."

Paul's honesty and healthy ambition inspire us in our pilgrimage. The wise person is the one who strives toward perfection in Christ. Although we may not be perfect, we are daily growing up into Christ. To do this, we, like Paul, must "be found in Him, not having mine own righteousness, which is of the law, but that which is through the faith of Christ."

Just honk

And if in any thing ye be otherwise minded,
God shall reveal even this unto you.
PHILIPPIANS 3:15

A Catholic priest told of driving behind a car with the message "Honk if you love Jesus" on a bumper sticker. "I don't exactly approve of that sort of thing," he said, "but maybe it was the nice weather or something." While stopping behind the car at a traffic light, the priest honked and waved. The lady in the car stuck out her head and yelled, "Can't you see the light is red, stupid?" The priest laughed and said, "It serves me right."

This incident reminds us that we often are tempted to act out of character with our Christian witness. In the heat of busy days we sometimes say or do things that are not a good testimony for the kingdom. The lady's attitude was wrong, and she probably later regretted it.

Paul squarely approached the problem of being human. He admonishes us always to act like believers and reminds us that when we do not, God can and will call this to our attention. If the lady driver was a sincere believer in Christ, she was convicted of her sin and asked forgiveness from Christ.

It is wonderful to realize that God loves us so much He demands our best. He makes us uncomfortable when we do wrong and tells us how to correct it. God's Word, Paul said, is "profitable for doctrine, for reproof, for correction, for instruction in righteousness" (2 Tim. 3:16).

Innocent victims

For our conversation is in heaven;
from whence also we look for the Saviour,
the Lord Jesus Christ.
PHILIPPIANS 3:20

The horror of Hitler often overshadows that of Mussolini. We must never forget, however, how evil this little dictator was. He marched without mercy on Ethiopia and machine-gunned peaceful people who still hunted with bows and arrows. He stayed in power for twenty-one years by murder, intrigue, and exile. When German forces collapsed in 1945, the escaping Mussolini was caught and, along with his mistress, shot. Their bodies were taken to Milan and hung by the heels in front of a garage. It was an ugly end to an ugly and totally immoral man.

There are evil men in the world and some even in the church. Paul warns the Philippians of some false teachers "whose end is destruction, whose God is their belly, and whose glory is in their shame, who mind earthly things." Their end, like Mussolini's, will be disgrace and damnation.

Pitted against the evil ones of this world are those who, like Paul, can say that their "conversation is in heaven." These are men who live for eternity rather than the few years between birth and the grave. They refuse to live by the law of the jungle – "Survival of the fittest" – but seek to fulfill their responsibilities to God and man. May our conversation be rooted in eternity rather than in the gutters of this earth.

Public rebuke

I beseech Euodias, and beseech Syntyche,
that they be of the same mind in the Lord.
PHILIPPIANS 4:2

The same day the disastrous Chicago fire broke out, a forest fire started in Peshtigo, Wisconsin, which killed five hundred more people than the Chicago blaze. Called the worst natural disaster in history, the Wisconsin fire started when many small fires were sparked in the dry weather. The Chicago conflagration received more publicity because it caused far more property damage and because of the romantic story of Mrs. O'Leary's cow beginning the Chicago blaze. The fact is, both fires were devastating.

Much attention had been given to the false prophets within the early church. However, Paul saw another potential danger to the young church – a disagreement between two ladies in the assembly. Apparently the feud had reached such proportions that it threatened to consume the little church. Paul insisted that drastic measures be taken.

Never one to back away from problems, Paul insisted that other believers help the ladies settle their differences. Often we need others to help us see our problem from a different viewpoint before we can solve it. We must remember that left unattended, our little fires of anger can bring destruction and even spiritual death.

The "thank-you cure"

*But in every thing by prayer and
supplication with thanksgiving let
your requests be made known unto God.*
PHILIPPIANS 4:6

A wise old doctor in South Wales often pre-
scribes the "thank-you cure". When a patient
comes to him depressed but without symp-
toms of serious woes, the doctor tells him,
"For six weeks I want you to say 'Thank you'
whenever someone does you a favor. And to
show you mean it, emphasize the words with
a smile." When the patient complains that few
do him favors, the doctor simply replies, "Seek
and ye shall find." Six weeks later the patient
returns with a new outlook, freed of his griev-
ances against life, convinced that people have
suddenly become more kind and friendly.

There is grace in gratitude. God's Word is filled with admonitions to thank Him for the things in our lives. This is where praise begins. The wise believer has learned to begin and end all prayers and supplications with thanksgiving. In doing so we are more aware of the goodness of God and the kindness of others.

Praise does far more for us than it does for God. Our Father is not some egocentric being who needs to be told constantly how wonderful He is. He desires the praise of His people because it opens their hearts to God and their fellow-man. The grateful heart is a gracious heart. We are to season our requests with thanksgiving, and in so doing our love for the Lord grows deeper.

Mind advertisement

———————— ⌒⌒⌒ ————————

For I have learned, in whatsoever
state I am, therewith to be content.
PHILIPPIANS 4:11

Famed author Bruce Barton has wisely said: "For good or ill, your conversation is your advertisement. Every time you open your mouth you let men look into your mind." Jesus said the same thing many years earlier: "for out of the abundance of the heart the mouth speaketh" (Matt. 12:34). It is true that to know how people think and what they are, we only need to listen to their words.

Take Paul, for example. The famous apostle said, "for I have learned, in whatsoever state I am, therewith to be content." Paul knew how to be abased and how to abound. In other words, the circumstances of his life did not affect his happiness. Rather, his joy was firmly rooted in a relationship with the Lord he loved. In such confidence Paul could frankly claim, "I can do all things through Christ which strengtheneth me."

It would be well to listen to ourselves talk today. Is our conversation laced with positive faith or negative doubt? Does it expose a mind that is thoroughly saturated in love for Christ or in the things of this world? Our strongest witness for Christ is a positive conversation that breathes hope.

The sea cares

No church communicated with me as concerning giving and receiving, but ye only.
PHILIPPIANS 4:15

At sunset a little girl sat with her father at the edge of the ocean watching the tide come in. The waves sent a sheet of molten gold across the dry sand, almost like a caress from the arms of the sea. In that magic moment the daughter said dreamily, "Isn't it wonderful how much the sea cares about the land." Telling about the incident, the father said, "She was right. The land was merely passive. But the sea cared – and so it came."

Caring costs. It means reaching out to help when others pass by. Paul knew the cost and comfort of such care. Philippi had been the only church that had seen his physical needs and relieved them. They would forever occupy a special place in his heart. He did not have to ask for their help. They saw and they reached out. Thus he promised them, "my God shall supply all your need according to His riches in glory by Christ Jesus."

Most of us say to someone in need, "If I can help, please tell me." The loving person does not even ask. He moves to relieve the person's needs and touch him with his concern. Caring does cost, but its rewards are eternal. May we look around today and really see the needs of others. Then may we relieve those needs in a practical and loving way. This brings blessing to both giver and receiver.

The pebble

The trying of your faith worketh patience.
JAMES 1:3

A small trouble is like a pebble," Celia Luce has said. "Hold it too close to your eye and it fills the whole world and puts everything out of focus. Hold it at the proper viewing distance, and it can be examined and properly classified. Throw it at your feet, and it can be seen in its true setting, just one more tiny bump on the pathway to eternity." Wise words from a wise woman.

James encourages us to keep trouble and even temptations in their proper perspective. In the sadness or passion of the moment, we often have them pressed to our face where we can see nothing else. They are constantly in our thoughts and overwhelm us. We need to cast them at our feet and remember God can and will use them to make us better believers. The trying of our faith does, as James said, produce patience.

Most of us are like the kindergartner who planted a tiny seed in a small flowerpot and dug it up every day to see how it was doing. We must learn to "let patience have her perfect work, that ye may be perfect and entire, wanting nothing." One believer joked, "I want patience and I want it right now." Too often we think like that. May we relax and put the pebbles of tribulation and temptation in their proper place. We need not be dominated by them, and through Christ we can conquer them.

In the teeth of death

If any of you lack wisdom, let him ask of God,
that giveth to all men liberally.
JAMES 1:5

In one hand I have a Bible, and in the other a pistol" the communist guard said, taunting Salvation Army Commissioner Herbert Lord. "I despise your God. Let me see you prove His power. Pray to Him to tell you which hand holds the Bible and which the gun. If you are wrong I will kill you." Lord lowered his head. "Have you prayed?" the guard asked. "Which hand did your God tell you?" "I did not ask," the Christian said. "For two things only I prayed: that God help me keep my temper and for strength to die decently." The guard's face twisted in anger and he took aim with his gun. Then, frustrated, he turned away.

50

The firm resolve of Commissioner Lord is shared by many believers in deep crisis. God has provided a resource to His children which no other humans have. When we face trials, James tells us to ask for divine wisdom and promises that God can and will give it. As the communist guard was frustrated, so the enemy of our souls will be by the wisdom Christ gives.

Although we are not facing a firing squad, the promise is still ours. If we but ask for spiritual direction, God will supply it. In every decision today may we seek His perfect will for us.

Died a grocer

Let the brother of low degree rejoice in that he is exalted: but the rich, in that he is made low.
JAMES 1:9-10

Asked to explain the meaning of an epitaph he had written for his tombstone – "Born, a Human Being; Died, a Wholesale Grocer" – the businessman replied, "I was so busy selling groceries I did not have time to get married and have a family. I was successful. But I was so busy making a living, I never had time to live." Many today have a similar problem.

James points out that life is just a vapor and we must spend our time doing important things. He reminds us that the man born in low circumstances can be exalted through Christ and that those born in riches should rejoice because they can enter the door of eternal salvation. The door is open to all men without preference. The only key is faith in Christ.

We often need to be reminded that we are creatures of eternity, not of time. We must consider our actions not in terms of our few short years on this globe, but of that day when we will stand before our Creator and account for the deeds of the flesh. May we constantly remember that we were born human beings and that we need not die in despair. Through Christ we can and will live forever. Let us not be so busy making a living that we forget to make a life.

Aversion therapy

But every man is tempted, when he is drawn away of his own lust, and enticed.

JAMES 1:14

Aversion therapy is a rapidly growing and intensely controversial way to change human behavior. This therapy rests on the premise that you can punish undesirable behavior over and over until the patient so links the behavior and the punishment that he gives up that behavior. Those who want to quit smoking are given electrical shocks every time they pick up a cigarette. The drinker who desires to stop is either shocked or so chemically treated that a drink makes him physically ill. This therapy does not attempt to get at the root of behavior; it merely conditions a person's actions.

While the new form of therapy sounds

good, it will never really work since change must come from within, not from external pressures. James pointedly said the problems of behavior spill over from the heart. Temptations are temptations only because the person has first been drawn away by his own lusts. Obviously the best therapy is to have a change of both heart and head through Christ.

Understanding this, the believer looks to Christ for inner strength against evil. Then there is something each of us can do: "Wherefore lay apart all filthiness and superfluity of naughtiness, and receive with meekness the engrafted word, which is able to save your souls" (James 1:21).

Men of action

But be ye doers of the word, and not
hearers only, deceiving your own selves.
JAMES 1:22

I want my religion like my tea – hot!" proclaimed General William Booth, founder of the Salvation Army. In 1865 he set up his first tiny mission for down-and-outers in London. Booth's officers used shock methods to win converts. They charged into gin palaces and dragged drunkards out. They gained public attention with all the tricks of a circus barker. One poster told of "men who were once wild as lions, savage as tigers … who were prowling through the black jungles of sin, but captured by our troops and tamed."

While one may disagree with Booth's methods, there is no doubt his efforts affected modern history. The Salvation Army is today a monument to a man so dedicated to his Christ that he did something about rescuing the perishing. James said that men of faith are men of action, not just of words.

In a colorful word picture, James noted that if we look into God's Word and do nothing about what we see there, we are like a man who looks into a mirror and then forgets what he saw. Practical Christianity involves doing something about cleaning up our own lives and reaching the lost.

Maybe we need a few more William Booths in our century, men who like their religion "hot" with active service to their Master. Real believers are not merely hearers; they are doers.

A bum's advice

But if ye have respect to persons,
ye commit sin, and are convinced
of the law as transgressors.
JAMES 2:9

Several years ago Alfred Hitchcock, the famous motion picture director, was on location in a New York slum when inclement weather brought the filming to a halt. A filthy old man sidled up to Hitchcock and said, "I have a suggestion. Why don't you rig up some artificial light?" Hitchcock patiently explained to the derelict why this was impossible, treating him with great respect. Asked about it later, Hitchcock said, "Ideas come from everywhere, including left field. You have to listen or you're lost."

This act went beyond kindness and took

account of human potential, however low the light is burning. James tells us that believers must treat all men alike. We are often so impressed with the rich that we forget they have hungry hearts like the rest of us. We are tempted to like them for what they have or who they are. Or we are so disgusted with the shabby that we turn them off. The wise believer realizes that both are God's children.

If we show preference for the rich, James warns, we transgress the law. Believers are to love all men alike. May we pray today to see men as men, not as types or in social brackets. This is real Christian love.

Critical dimensions

*For as the body without the spirit is dead,
so faith without works is dead also.*
JAMES 2:26

In building the huge Arch of St. Louis, dimensions were so critical that surveyors had to work at night when the temperatures on all three walls were the same. Each measurement had to be exact. In pouring the foundation of either leg, a mistake of only 1/64 of an inch would have been disastrous. That difference in the angle of the top of each foundation would be multiplied until the two fingers reaching toward the sky would have failed to meet. All of the careful work was worth it, and the arch today is a fitting monument to the opening of the West and to the ingenuity of man.

Like the two towers of the Arch, faith and

works reach toward each other. In church history there have been miscalculations as to the importance of each. Some emphasized works so much that the Reformation had to call Christendom back to faith. On the other hand, mere faith is not enough, James said. Both legs of the tower must meet for the structure to be complete.

Theologians will continue to disagree on the proper balance of faith and works. While the battle rages, we laymen merely need to ask God's Holy Spirit to help us maintain a proper balance of faith and works. Faith and works can be combined in proper proportion to where our lives will be monuments of blessings.

Little things

Out of the same mouth proceedeth
blessing and cursing. My brethren,
these things ought not so to be.
JAMES 3:10

Little things can mean a lot. The jerking of a panful of frogs' legs when touched by a knife led to the discovery of dynamic electricity. The trembling lid of a teakettle was the beginning of the steam engine. A spider's web across the corner of a garden inspired the suspension bridge. A lantern swinging from the dome of a cathedral suggested the principle of the pendulum, by which time is measured. An apple falling from a tree revealed the law of gravity. And a cow kicking over a lantern caused the devastating Chicago fire.

James considered little things so important that he spent almost a whole chapter talking about the destructive fires of evil the tongue can ignite. He said frankly, "If any man offend not in word, the same is a perfect man, and able also to bridle the whole body." He warned that believers cannot continue to spew forth words of blessing and of cursing. The conversation of the Christian is changed at conversion.

We are eternally at war with our tongue. It is like a wild and untamed horse that we must ride constantly to keep it from disrupting and destroying relationships. Today it would be well to give special attention to this powerful instrument. While we each ask God for a thousand tongues to praise our great Redeemer, let us each control the one we have.

Two steps behind

From whence come wars and fightings among you? Come they not hence, even of your lusts that war in your members?
JAMES 4:1

The chief tragedy of the human race," Sydney J. Harris says, "is that the war approaching always seems necessary and inevitable. It is only 20 years later that it is seen as avoidable and futile. Is the mind perpetually condemned to live two steps behind the passions?" Tragically it seems so, even in our modern society. Lewis Mumford, historian and philosopher, says, "The dark age is not coming – we are in the midst of the dark age."

Nowhere else in literature is there such a clear statement of the cause of all wars as the Book of James. James pinpointed the source of all conflicts, whether they be personal, ecclesiastical, or national: the lusts in our hearts. War will be with us until our hearts change.

While historians might think James's statement too simplistic, perhaps we should consider all battles in the light of the apostle's statement. On a personal level we find that conflicts arise from selfishness or insistence on our own way. According to James, friendship with such a worldly spirit is enmity with God. If we are friends with this type of spirit, we are enemies of God. May our desires be tempered today with His will, and then our lives will not spill over into feuds and fights, but will bring healing to men.

What can I do?

Draw nigh to God, and he
will draw nigh to you.
JAMES 4:8

During the recent energy crises we seemed so helpless. Then the New York Daily News showed how each of us could save energy: "One less hour a day of color TV saves a fourth barrel of oil a year. One less washing machine load saves a half barrel. One less clothes dryer load saves a third barrel. Using the dishwasher once for every two present uses saves three and a half barrels, while using the air conditioner one less hour from May through September saves a half barrel." There is something we can do.

James tells the believer some things he can do to make his life more like Christ's. While

Jesus is the Author and Finisher of our faith, there are practical steps we can take to be more aware of His working and more suitable to His service. James suggests, for example, that we submit ourselves to God and resist the devil, that we draw near to God so that He will draw near to us.

James adds that we should not speak evil of one another or say arrogantly that we will do as we please. We are in God's hands, not ours. We are to do good because "to him that knoweth to do good, and doeth it not, ... it is sin." With such a list we have a lot to work on today in our lives. There is something we can do, and may we do it.

The rocking chair

*The effectual fervent prayer of
a righteous man availeth much.*
JAMES 5:16

A woman who reared a large family and ran a boarding house at the same time was asked how she remained so composed. "Well," she said, "you know that big rocking chair in my room? Every afternoon, no matter how busy I am, I go up there to rock awhile and empty out my brains." While this is good therapy, there comes a time when we need to do more than empty out our brains; we need to empty our souls. This is why James closed his important letter with a strong admonition to pray.

Prayer is far more than pouring out our woes. We do not speak to the air when we make our petitions. There is One who listens and is touched by our infirmities. Therefore, to keep a healthy spiritual life we must consider prayer our privilege and responsibility.

James 5:16 tells us to pray if we are afflicted, to seek prayer from our brothers and sisters in the Lord for our illnesses and problems. James also reminds us that Elijah was a man of prayer who suffered the same frustration we do. What marked him as a great man of God was his practice of prayer. Indeed, "the effectual fervent prayer of a righteous man availeth much." Today may we be ones who pray. Only then will we accomplish great things for the kingdom.

Surprising statistics

"And take heed to yourselves, lest at any time your hearts be overcharged with surfeiting, and drunkenness, and cares of this life."
LUKE 21:34

While we Americans complain about the soaring food prices, we pay a smaller percentage of our income for food than people of other nations. Statistics released by the New York Times indicate that Americans spend approximately 17.6 percent of their income for food, as opposed to 21.9 for Germans, 26.5 for the French, and 22.3 for the Japanese. Other peoples of the world are even more desperate. In India 60 percent of a person's income goes for food, while in some parts of Africa, 70 percent.

Life in an affluent society raises unique

problems. Americans must decide how to use their money wisely. This is no problem in countries like India and Africa where necessity dictates. But we must remember that, as Jesus said, much is required of the one who has been given much.

Christ's words of warning in Luke 21:34 are most appropriate for the West. In the last days we are tempted to waste our substance rather than use it wisely. Jesus told us to shun excess, drunkenness, and the cares of this world. In our materialistic society we are to maintain a proper perspective and look for His coming.

Best investment

*For the word of God is quick, and powerful,
and sharper than any two-edged sword.*
HEBREWS 4:12

When John Wanamaker was eleven years old, he bought a Bible. In later years he said, "I have made many large purchases in my time involving millions of dollars. But the purchase of that Bible was my greatest buy. I paid for it in small installments. Looking back over my life I see that little book was the foundation on which my life has been built, and the thing that has made possible all that has counted in my life. I know now it was my greatest investment and the most far reaching and important purchase I ever made."

Wise men recognize the value of God's Word. In prayer we speak to God, and through

His Word He speaks to us. The writer of Hebrews said God's Word is quick and powerful, sharper than any double-edged sword, "piercing even to the dividing asunder of soul and spirit, and of the joints and marrow, and [it] is a discerner of the thoughts and intents of the heart."

James called the Word a mirror. In it we see ourselves and also what we can be in Christ. By reading the pages of Holy Writ, we grow up into Christ in all things. The sincere believer will make God's Word part of his daily diet. Even though parts of the Bible may be hard to read, it is best if we read all parts. May we vow today to carry His Word with us and use it every day.

Denial

Lord, I believe; help thou mine unbelief.
MARK 9:24

Bennet Cerf tells about the London plutocrat who, driving his new Rolls Royce through the Alps, heard a disquieting snap. The front spring had broken. He called the Rolls plant, and they flew a new spring to him as well as mechanics to install it. Six months passed and the Londoner received no bill. He went to the plant and asked about it. After a brief delay the manager appeared, gazed at him reproachfully, and announced, "There must be some mistake, sir. There is no such thing as a broken spring on a Rolls Royce."

Many people treat doubt as the plant manager did the broken spring. They deny its existence and try to talk themselves into some pseudofaith. This seldom works, however. A better way of handling doubt is that of the father who brought his child to Jesus to be healed. When Christ asked, "Do you believe?" the man admitted, "I believe; help Thou mine unbelief." His child was healed.

Jesus honored the man's request because he lived in the arena of his faith rather than the house of his doubt. He had come to Jesus even though he did have his doubt. God understood and healed. Honesty is always the best policy. If we open our hearts frankly to the Lord, He always hears and heals.

Love at home

*Nevertheless let every one of you in particular
so love his wife even as himself; and
the wife see that she reverence her husband.*
EPHESIANS 5:33

Legend tells of an attractive young couple who boarded a train for the traditional honeymoon at Niagara Falls. They were very much in love, and that was apparent to all who saw them. Suddenly the bride found herself hurling insults at her husband and his rejoinders matched hers in bitterness and venom. Then she discovered a stranger sitting next to her whose presence had caused the transformation. "How did you get in here?" she gasped. "And who are you?" The stranger softly answered, "I'm Ten-years-from-now."

Many marriages are under stresses that

threaten to destroy them. The sweetness of the honeymoon has worn off, and the business of living has caused some abrasions. Paul understood these problems, and he spent much time admonishing husbands and wives. Here is his formula for a happy home and a lasting marriage.

There must be one leader in the home, and God ordained the man to be that. But the man has a spiritual obligation to deeply love his wife as his own body. Both are to cling to each other rather than side against each other with relatives. The admonition to love is so strong that Paul repeated it again and likened the husband-wife relationship to that of Christ and His Church. In today's prayer period, let us pray for a deeper love in our homes.

From us

Cee

Cast thy bread upon the waters:
for thou shalt find it after many days.
ECCLESIASTES 11:1

Two shipwrecked men were marooned on an uninhabited island in the South Pacific. They had been there for many months, living off roots and berries, when they saw a bottle floating in on the tide. They shrieked with joy. With trembling hands they uncorked it to get the note inside. When they saw the note, their faces fell. "Nuts," one of them exclaimed. "It's from us." This illustrates that whatever we throw out will eventually come back to us. This is the premise of Ecclesiastes 11:1. The farmer's fields were flooded, but he sowed anyway. When the waters receded, the seed grew and the crop came.

There is an eternal law of sowing and reaping. If we are merciful, we obtain mercy. If we sow to the flesh, we, like the flesh, are destined for corruption. If we sow to the spirit, we receive eternal life. Therefore, we continue to sow good seeds for the kingdom although it now seems fruitless to do so. Solomon was wise in saying, "In the morning sow thy seed, and in the evening withhold not thine hand: for thou knowest not whether shall prosper, either this or that, or whether they both shall be alike good." Our job is to sow faith; it is God's job to make the crop grow.

No longer blind

*One thing I know, that, whereas
I was blind, now I see.*
JOHN 9:25

A Virginia woman is now able to see for the first time in seventy years. Josephine Mulkey had been blind since an accident at age six. A recent operation, however, restored vision to her and she said, "It makes me so happy that I feel like singing 'How Great Thou Art.'" One of the most pleasant surprises, said Mrs. Mulkey, was seeing what a beautiful family she had raised. Her grandchildren and neighbors had looked much like she expected "but much prettier." She added, "Everything I look at is so pretty."

The ecstasy Mrs. Mulkey experienced is the same felt by the man who, having been blind from birth, was healed by Christ. The man was so enraptured by the new world around him that he was totally uninterested in the accusations of Jesus' enemies. He answered their accusations with this: "Whether He be a sinner or no, I know not: one thing I know, that, whereas I was blind, now I see."

We who have been released from spiritual blindness get impatient with the critics of Christ. Our personal experience tells us that He indeed is the Messiah, and the arguments of the agnostics and the atheists seem silly to us. We once sat in darkness, but now we have seen a great light. When we experience something, we are never at the mercy of those who argue against it.

Sing a song

*Let every thing that hath breath
praise the Lord. Praise ye the Lord.*
PSALM 150:6

Tradition tells us that Ambrose, the fighting bishop of Milan, introduced singing into the European church. In A.D. 380 the church was rent with heresy, and the devout kept "watch day and night in the church, ready to die with their bishop ... singing hymns and psalms so they would not succumb to weariness and grief." Today we have more than 400,00 hymns in the English language, and new ones are being written every day. God's Word tells us we are to praise God in song.

Much of Christianity's vitality lies in its hymns. When we get together for worship and sing unto the Lord, His Spirit draws us to Himself. Charles Wesley, a great hymnist, knew the power of sacred song. In his pocket hymnal he tells us how we should sing: "Sing all. Join with the congregation as frequently as you can. Let not weariness nor weakness hinder you. Sing lustily with a good courage. Above all, sing spiritually. Have an eye to God in every word you sing. Aim at pleasing Him more than yourself. So shall your singing be such as the Lord will approve of."

This is good advice for us. God desires that we worship Him in song. "Let every thing that hath breath praise the Lord. Praise ye the Lord." Today is a day to sing praises to our Savior.

Hunger

"And there shall be famines, and pestilences, and earthquakes, in diverse places."
MATTHEW 24:7

Observers predict that within a few years the most crucial issue will be hunger. Because world demand for food is rising rapidly, our ninety-day stockpile in this country has dwindled to one for twenty-seven days. Scientists predict that one major crop failure would result in the worst famine this world has ever known. Adding to the problem is the unequal distribution of food: the average person in poor countries consumes about four hundred pounds of grain a year; the average North American eats about a ton, at least one hundred pounds of which is in the form of whiskey and beer.

James Reston says, "The rich world doesn't really believe in the coming food crisis any more than it believes in the oil crisis. One day we will all be weight watchers." A famine is already spreading in Africa, and the hunger in India has long been known. Famine should not surprise believers since Jesus foresaw it, predicting an increase of famine before His return.

Our world is desperate. In these troubled times the believer must not panic and seek shelter from the hurts of humanity. He must go forth to share the Christ who can solve these problems and guide man through the trying days ahead. Christ is coming soon!

Caring counts

*The Lord give mercy unto the house
of Onesiphorus; for he oft refreshed me,
and was not ashamed of my chain.*
2 TIMOTHY 1:16

A famous jeweler once sold a magnificent ruby to a customer after one of his salesmen had failed. Asked how he did it, the jeweler said, "My clerk is an excellent man and also an expert on precious stones. There is just one difference between us. He knows jewels, but I love them. I care what happens to them and who wears them. The customers sense this. It makes them want to buy – and they do." Not only with jewels but with all aspects of life, caring counts.

Paul, writing his last will and testament to young Timothy, praised Onesiphorus and asked that Timothy greet him. This young man had sought out Paul while he was in prison. Onesiphorus was not ashamed of Paul's chains and spent time encouraging him. He did this not just out of Christian duty, but out of a real love for the Lord and for Paul. His caring counted.

Today we will probably be asked to perform some act of Christian love for our church, our neighbors, or our families. May we learn to do these things not just because they are expected of us but because we really care, and may we convey that to those to whom we minister. People can sense when we really are concerned for their spiritual welfare and not just interested in them as a statistic or out of duty. May we strive today to be an Onesiphorus.

Selfless

―――――― ⟨Ɵɾ⟩ ――――――

"Ye are my friends, if ye do
whatsoever I command you."
JOHN 15:14

The plane carrying Dr. Frederick Banting,
a famous physician-scientist, crashed in a
snowstorm in a forest near Musgrave Harbor,
Newfoundland. One of Banting's lungs was
punctured by crushed ribs, but he used his
waning strength to bandage the wounds of
the pilot, the only survivor. Then he lay down
on the pine boughs in the snow and went into
the sleep from which he never awakened. This
great doctor who had done so much for humanity by discovering insulin died as he had
lived, in selfless service to others.

Jesus talked of such men: "Greater love
hath no man than this, that a man lay down

his life for his friends." Jesus Himself later did this, sacrificing His life for all the sins of this world. We admire men like Banting, but we adore Christ because He was not a mere man; He was God's only Son who came to die that we might live.

The premise of the gospel Christ preached is that we should selflessly serve Him. Jesus often talked of crosses to carry, burdens to bear, and enemies to love. He then said that if we obey His commands, we are indeed His friend and He ours. Love is not optional with the believer, however. "This is My commandment, that ye love one another, as I have loved you." The real believer is one who has given up his own selfishness to serve Christ and those about him. We are saved to serve.

Destiny

"Before I formed thee in the belly I knew thee."
JEREMIAH 1:5

Perhaps the most moving eulogy of Dr. Frederick Banting was one given at a gathering of the Diabetics Association: "Without Banting this meeting could have only been a gathering of ghosts bemoaning their fate." Dr. Banting was the main one responsible for the discovery of insulin which has extended the lives of million of diabetics. Because Dr. Banting fulfilled his destiny, the world is a much better place in which to live.

God spoke explicitly to a young man centuries ago and told him his destiny. God said to Jeremiah: "Before I formed thee in the belly I knew thee; and before thou camest forth out of the womb I sanctified thee, and

I ordained thee a prophet unto the nations." If Jeremiah had balked and refused to fulfill his destiny, we probably never would have known about Daniel and the three Hebrew children. All four were deeply influenced by Jeremiah's life.

God gives us the choice either to accept or reject our destiny. In Romans Paul said that God desires us to be conformed to the image of His Son. This is our destiny. If we move with it, our world will be a warmer and finer place to live. If we balk, many may fail to hear of our Lord and, like the diabetics, will be merely a gathering of ghosts bemoaning their fate.

Courtesy

_Finally, be ye all of one mind, having
compassion one of another, love
as brethren, be pitiful, be courteous._
1 PETER 3:8

When actor Lloyd Bridges and his wife traveled East for a Broadway play, they left their fourteen-year-old son with friends. Mrs. Bridges says she was amazed and delighted to hear reports of how mannerly her son was being, but their first night home caused doubts. "He kept his head six inches from his place, talked with his mouth full and ate his cake and ice cream with his knife. 'Son, I can't imagine what the Browns were talking about,' his father exclaimed. 'Your manners are horrible.' 'Gee, Dad!' sputtered our son, 'You don't think I eat this way when I'm with people!'"

Too often we tend to forget our manners at home. We must remember, however, that God's Word encourages us to be courteous even there. Any home where "Thank you" or "Please excuse me" are heard frequently is a pleasant home and fulfills at least one Bible admonition – Peter said we are to be just as concerned for the comfort of our family as for anyone.

Christian courtesy includes having compassion for one another, loving each other as brethren, being full of pity, and refusing to hurt back when we are hurt or yell back when we are yelled at. Peter's advice is very practical to homemakers. And as a married person himself he knew the pitfalls and problems.

Empathy

—————— ⟨ℓℓℓℓ⟩ ——————

Rejoice with them that do rejoice,
and weep with them that weep.
ROMANS 12:15

Not long ago a minister had to tell the parents of a twelve-year-old boy that he had drowned on a school outing. Later the parents told about that moment: "Rev. Allen didn't preach to us or tell us to be brave. He broke into tears and wept with us. We will always love him for that." This was the spirit Paul captured when he admonished believers to "rejoice with them that do rejoice, and weep with them that weep."

So many of us are afraid to show sentiment. Yet throughout God's Word are examples of great men who were moved to tears. David is the most vivid example, and even Christ

94

wept over the city of Jerusalem. The Psalmist said, "They that sow in tears shall reap in joy. He that goeth forth and weepeth, bearing precious seed, shall doubtless come again with rejoicing, bringing his sheaves with him" (Ps. 126:5-6).

We should resolve to show our sentiment today, as the opportunity arises. With those who have been most fortunate and are basking in the joy of recent accomplishments or blessings may we sincerely rejoice and thank God. With those whose hearts have been broken may we share their grief, feeling deeply for them and reaching out to them in love.

No news

But the natural man receiveth not the
things of the Spirit of God: for they are
foolishness unto him: neither can he know
them, because they are spiritually discerned.
1 Corinthians 2:14

If newspapers would give less attention to
crime, there would not be so much of it,"
the average person on street says. In response
to requests from civic groups and individu-
als who felt that vandals were doing it for the
publicity, the news media in Iowa decided not
to report any news of vandalism for ninety
days. Then the police department released
statistics showing 36.5 percent more vandalism than during the same three months of the
year before.

Three things emerged from this experiment: first, turning one's back on a problem does not make it go away; second, an uninformed public often harbors a false sense of security; third, that which "sounds" logical is not always logical.

These three observations are also true in the spiritual realm. Turning our back on coming judgment does not erase that judgment.

The Bible says, "the soul that sinneth, it shall die." We also can be lured into a false sense of security through being ill informed about eternal values. And finally, "There is a way which seemeth right unto a man, but the end thereof are the ways of death" (Prov. 14:12). Natural man simply cannot perceive the things of God; only after we are born again do we have the proper perspective.

Foxhole

He that dwelleth in the secret place
of the most High shall abide under
the shadow of the Almighty.
PSALM 91:1

During the last days of World War II, President Harry S. Truman was asked how he managed to bear up so calmly under the stress and strain of the Presidency. He answered that he had "a foxhole in my mind," and just as a soldier retreats into his foxhole for protection and respite, Truman periodically retreated into his own "mental foxhole" where he allowed nothing to bother him. He had taken the advice of Marcus Aurelius: "Constantly then give to thyself this retreat, and renew thyself."

While Truman's mental foxhole might have been a good retreat, there is an even better one "under the shadow of the Almighty." Psalm 91, one of the most beloved chapters of the Bible, tells of the place of security to which the believer can go. In this spiritual foxhole, nothing can harm or hurt him. The Psalmist said that God "is my refuge and my fortress … in Him will I trust."

There are in our world some very real dangers. Not only are there physical dangers, there are spiritual ones. Even the most bold need the protection mentioned in this beautiful psalm, protection from "the terror by night, … the arrow that flieth by day, … the pestilence that walketh in darkness [and] … the destruction that wasteth at noonday."

Reaching out

─────── ⟨∾∾∾⟩ ───────

Let brotherly love continue.
HEBREWS 13:1

Often people ask Dr. Thomas P. Malone, a psychiatrist, what psychiatry is all about. His answer is, "Almost every emotional problem can be summed up in one particular bit of behavior – it's people walking around screaming 'for God's sake, love me.' He goes through a million different manipulations to get somebody to love him. On the other hand, healthy people are those who walk around looking for someone to love. And if you see changes in the people seeking for love, they give up their screaming for all their lives."

Dr. Malone's view of his role as a psychiatrist is certainly a noble and awesome one. He tries to get people to love one another. While psychiatry certainly has helped some to adjust, only Christ can so revolutionize character as to change a person from seeking to giving. Jesus came to this world to show men how to live. Through Christ we can learn how to give up our selfish seeking for attention and start giving ourselves to His kingdom.

Jesus told us that when we give up our lives, we find them. As we give up our selfish seeking and long to reach out in genuine love, we receive many blessings. No wonder it says in Hebrews, "Let brotherly love continue."

Partners

---

*Be fruitful and multiply, and replenish
the earth, and subdue it.*
GENESIS 1:28

A small department in a large company was producing less than it should have. The management finally went to the employees and said, "Consider yourselves a partnership. Here is your budget for personnel. Hire who you want and divide the money as you want. Just get the job done." The workers did just that and efficiency so increased that their salaries increased twenty-five percent. The point of the experiment was clear; a partnership works better than a pyramid in the business world.

In the very first chapter of the Bible we are told that we are in partnership with God. While God created the heavens and the earth,

He left it to man to subject the earth. Note His instructions to Adam: "Be fruitful, and multiply, and replenish the earth, and subdue it." As the company did with their employees, God has done with us. He has given us ample talent and resources to subdue this earth and to be fruitful and multiply. We can only do this, however, through a right relationship with God.

Throughout Scripture we are reminded of our partnership with God. In prayer we are His partners. As we pray, His will is done on earth. We bind and we loose by our prayers. We are His representatives in witness. God did not send angels to tell the story of Christ; He sent us into all the world. We are workers together with God.

Building

For if these things be in you, and abound,
they make you that ye shall neither
be barren nor unfruitful in the
knowledge of our Lord Jesus Christ.

2 PETER 1:8

The Ozark Mountain people have a saying: "A man don't know nothing he hasn't learned." In other words, we all start from the same level and build. Even genius depends on the data given it. William Shakespeare used playbooks to write his masterpieces. Mozart is said to have taken the opening theme of the overture *The Magic Flute* from a Clementi sonata. This does not diminish the genius of these men. It merely points out that their work stemmed from that of their predecessors.

In our work with the Lord, we must remember that every day is a building process in our lives. We are learning how to walk with Him. We were not born into the kingdom fully grown. In 2 Peter 1:8 Peter talked about the building process. He implied that we all start on the same level and "build" daily.

Our building materials are virtues such as faith, knowledge, and temperance. Others are patience, godliness, brotherly kindness, and charity. Peter said that as we give these virtues full sway in our lives we are fruitful, and as we ignore them we are barren. Peter's plea is clear: "Wherefore the rather, brethren, give diligence to make your calling and election sure: for if ye do these things, ye shall never fall" (2 Pet. 1:10).

Time

To every thing there is a season, and a time
to every purpose under the heaven.
ECCLESIASTES 3:1

Ardis Whitman tells of the death of a farmer's wife. She had been a good and busy mother, raising a family and toiling through the long days. At her funeral her husband did not weep, but he shuffled up to the pastor with a worn book in his hand. He said, "It's poems. She liked them. Would you read one for her now? She always wanted us to read them together, but I never had the time. Every day on the farm there were always things to do. But I got to thinking, nobody's doing them today and it doesn't seem to matter. I guess you don't get it into your head what time's for until it's too late."

Most of us abuse time rather than use it. The philosopher noted that when God made water He made it by the oceanfuls. He made flowers by the fieldfuls and stars by the heavenfuls. When He made time, however, He made it in day-tight compartments. We are wise if we learn to use time properly.

The Psalmist prayed, "So teach us to number our days, that we may apply our hearts unto wisdom" (90:12). We all feel guilty about our misuse of time. Let us ask God to give us a proper perspective on time. He can give us the wisdom to balance our time properly between our Lord, our family, our church, and our friends.

Soldier

Thou therefore endure hardness,
as a good soldier of Jesus Christ.
2 TIMOTHY 2:3

In 1919 President Woodrow Wilson pro-claimed November 11 as Armistice Day to remind Americans of the tragedies of war. In 1971 Congress changed the date to the fourth Monday in October and the name to Veterans Day. Canada has set aside a similar day – Remembrance Day on November 11. Both countries seek to show appreciation for all who gave their service and their lives for the lands we love.

It is sad that there even have to be veterans. Veterans are made by wars, and wars mar the history of mankind. Yet war will be with us as long as man is in rebellion against God.

Paul talks about another war being waged in the spirit world. The forces of Satan are pitted against the forces of our Lord and Christ. Paul admonished Timothy to be a good soldier for Christ and to endure hardness.

Christ never promised roses on the battle-field. We are involved in an intense spiritual warfare, and we will at times get weary. When it seems Satan has hit us with every weapon, we need to draw strength from Paul's words: "If we suffer, we shall also reign" with Christ (2 Tim. 2:12).

Snakebite

⟨⟨⟩⟩

And he shook off the beast into
the fire, and felt no harm.
ACTS 28:5

How the body digests food was first discovered on Michigan's Mackinac Island. A worker for the American Fur Company was accidentally shot in the stomach while shopping at an island store in 1822. Fort Mackinac's Dr. William Beaumont managed to save the young man's life, but the wound would not heal. As a result the doctor was able to observe and later to experiment with the previously unknown process of digestion. Those experiments greatly advanced medical knowledge.

Even unpleasant things have their rewards. Paul, shipwrecked on an island in the middle of the Mediterranean, was gathering sticks for a fire. Suddenly a snake bit him, and by all human understanding Paul should have died. Yet God refused to let the snake harm the apostle, and because of that event the islanders found the Lord. God brought something beautiful out of Paul's pain.

A poem says:

> Two men looked between the bars;
> One saw the mud, the other saw stars.

This is especially meaningful for believers. No matter what happens to us, we need only relax and let God glorify Himself through it. We need not panic. God is still on the throne. Let us look today at the stars and leave the mud for those without faith.